A World of Families

Trish Holland

TeachingStrategies® · Bethesda, MD

For Teaching Strategies, LLC.
Publisher: Larry Bram
Editorial Director: Hilary Parrish Nelson
VP Curriculum and Assessment: Cate Heroman
Product Manager: Kai-leé Berke
Book Development Team: Sherrie Rudick and Jan Greenberg
Project Manager: Jo A. Wilson

For Q2AMedia
Editorial Director: Bonnie Dobkin
Editor and Curriculum Adviser: Suzanne Barchers
Program Manager: Gayatri Singh
Creative Director: Simmi Sikka
Project Manager: Santosh Vasudevan
Designer: Ritu Chopra
Picture Researcher: Judy Brown

Picture Credits
t-top b-bottom c-center l-left r-right

Cover: Masterfile, Rasch/Shutterstock, Masterfile.

Back Cover: Lucian Coman/Dreamstime.

Title page: Photostogo: t, Ariel Skelley/Photolibrary: b.

Insides: Yvonne Chamberlain/Istockphoto: 3, Tetra Images/Photolibrary: 4, Masterfile: 5t, Lucian Coman/Dreamstime: 5b, Martha Cooper/Photolibrary: 6t, Monkey Business Images/Dreamstime: 6b, H Vibhu/The Hindu: 7, Corbis/Photolibrary: 8, Photostogo: 9t, Masterfile: 9b, Nigel Pavitt/Photolibrary: 10t, Masterfile: 10b, Masterfile: 11, Masterfile: 12, Carson Ganci/Photolibrary: 13l, Masterfile: 13r, Ariel Skelley/Photolibrary: 14t, Ma Mo Pictures/Istockphoto: 14b, Masterfile: 15, Tetra Images/Photolibrary: 16, Wsphotos/Istockphoto: 17t, Masterfile: 17b, Masterfile: 18, Jim Parkin/Dreamstime: 19, Photostogo: 20, Heiner Heine/Photolibrary: 21t, Masterfile: 21b, Masterfile: 22, Panorama Media/Photolibrary: 23, Istockphoto: 24.

Teaching Strategies, LLC.
Bethesda, MD
www.TeachingStrategies.com

ISBN: 978-1-60617-142-4

Library of Congress Cataloging-in-Publication Data
Holland, Trish.
  A world of families / Trish Holland.
    p. cm.
  ISBN 978-1-60617-142-4
  1. Family--Juvenile literature. I. Title.
  HQ744.H55 2010
  306.85--dc22
                          2009037266
CPSIA tracking label information:
RR Donnelley, Shenzhen, China
Date of Production: Nov 2016
Cohort: Batch 6

Printed and bound in China

8 9 10	17 16
Printing	Year Printed

Families around the world come
in all sizes and combinations.

Even though they look
different, families like and
do many of the same things.

The people in families eat together.

They play sports and games together.

They go places together.

Some families even work together!

Families sing, dance, and make music together.

They read to each other and tell stories.

They carry on family traditions.

They celebrate family events.

When holidays come, families gather with grandparents, aunts, uncles, and cousins. On those days, families make special memories.

The people in families around the world love and care for each other, just as the people in your family love and care for you.